Planet Earth

THE THREE INN KEEPERS

Patrick O'Neill

Llumina
PRESS

ISBN: 978-1-62550-360-2

Printed in the United States of America by Llumina Press

Acknowledgements/Credits

Cover: oil on canvas: Grady O'Neill.

Illustrations for "Wolves, Deer, and Notions" and for "Between a Canoe and a Dock" Bill O'Neill.
Photographs for "Bridges: Kristy O'Neill.

Thanks to the publishers and editors of the following periodicals:

Parting Gifts for publishing "Possum."
Phoebe for publishing "Verse in Need of Revision."

Prologue

The niece of the narrator of "Roots, Feathers, Skin, fur, Scales—and a Poem"—daughter of the narrator's sister, the botanist—with input from both the narrator and his sister, wrote the poem "Soil, Water, and Sky" for her freshman comp class and received an "A-" on it. The poem is a key player in the plot of the Primary poem "Roots, Feathers, Skin, Fur, Scales—and a Poem." It also reflects a major focus of the overall revelations of the poetry of this book—*Planet Earth: The Three Inn Keepers.*

The Poem:

Soil, Water, and Sky:

generate the energy,

provide the living

and the dying accommodations

for tenants that bud, bloom,

crawl, walk, swim, and fly.

We human beings establish
ourselves as superior,
point our noses at the sky.

We wander, flounder, and trek
among the planet's many mysteries,
assaults, and temptations
till we—reluctantly—die.

These are not lines;

they're stanzas!

A-

(From: "Roots, Feathers, Skin, Fur, Scales—and a
Poem." *Planet Earth: The Three Innkeepers*

Contents

Planet Earth

THE THREE INN KEEPERS

Shut Up

Shut up before you speak. Shut up
while you're speaking, after you speak.
When you rev up and take off, watch for stop signs,
red lights, red blinkers. Look out!
There's a comma. Shut up.
Here comes a semicolon. Shut up—
a dash, colon, period, question mark,
an exclamation mark. Shut up; shut up.
Indentation coming at you, the end
of your dissertation. Shut up. Hand Silence
the mic. Kick your mind off the restraints
of trivial noise and let Silence engage—
travel, explore, and discover. Silence speaks
with more resolve, sincerity, dynamics than noise.

Decades ago: I stand with my back to a class
scribbling grammatical trivia on the black board.
I walk from the board toward the window—
my wearying voice trailing remnants of the trivia
behind me when—KABLAST—a huge explosion

annihilates the trivia, the passivity. Fragments
of the blackboard, carrying my tired scribbling,
shoot like grenade shrapnel out over my desk,
striking the floor just short of front-row students.
After squeals, screams—hurried scrapes
of desks as some students make a break
for the door—a heavy silence surrounds us,
smacks us with wonderment, presentiment, relief.
That profound silence and the passion-fostered
words that soon float from it like songs
always will carry a throng more decibels
than the kablast of the shattering blackboard.
That terse explosion of silence would echo
in our adventures, our misadventures for decades.

Postscript:

The shattering of the blackboard that happened in the
sixties and inspired the poem was a mystery for hours.
We eventually correlated it with a sonic boom that we
in the classroom couldn't discern because of the
shattering of the board. After a military lawyer and Air
Force Captain jetted from Washington, interrogated
my class and me, and studied the evidence for a
couple months, they sent the school a check for
something less than a hundred bucks. That gave the

school board some incentive to consider the matter—
and eventually give the go ahead to the maintenance
crew to replace the section of the blackboard that
exploded and could have killed me and seriously
injured my students. The missing center section of the
blackboard became a symbol of that memorable blast
of silence that followed the shattering of the board
and brought meaning and energy to the classroom for
the remainder of the semester. I didn't mark the new
board with my tired chalk scrawls after it came. I left
it empty to continue shouting its profound silence at
the class and me for the one final week—and beyond.

Listen:

Eleva, Wisconsin

In a small Wisconsin settlement,
Winter chased away the "tor."
Intending to finish in the spring,
the painters hung up their brushes
when the cold and snow threatened
and they never did finish the job.
When the Town's founders wandered in,
they picked the town's name
from the partially painted grain elevator.
There is an up and a down to it.
They picked the wrong syllables.
Eleva's on the lower level.
They should have used the syllable
that wasn't there. "Tor"*
has more clout than "Eleva."

because it narrates those endeavors

that hardship chases us away from—

the most vital and challenging—

the most elevated.

*Tor: a high, rocky/craggy hill.

Wolves, Deer, and Notions

I cross the Montreal River Bridge,

connecting the Upper Peninsula

of Michigan to northern Wisconsin—

Ironwood, Michigan to Hurley, Wisconsin—

to visit Nora's Bar. I spot a friend

at the far end of the bar. He's a guy

who somehow, somewhere digs up

and swears by the damnedest notions. I find

a stool next to him, park on it. He nods at me.

I order a beer and wait. Like he usually does,

he looks at the back bar for a while.

I'm never sure if he's recalling or inventing.

I suspect both—mixing together

what he invents and what he recalls.

He finally says, It's funny how everyone

is down on the environmental groups

for promoting the protection and propagation

of wolves in—he swings his hand in the direction

of Michigan—the U.P. Why? *I ask*. They're losing

livestock—even pets to wolves. Yeah, *he says*.

But it's not the environmental groups

who are really pushing it. They don't have

enough clout. Who is it then? *I ask*.

It's the goddamned insurance companies.

Car-deer accidents are costing them a bundle:

simple logic—the more wolves to kill them,

the fewer deer—the fewer collisions,

the fewer insurance checks. When a car hits a deer,

there's only one party the insurance company

can hit for compensation for their liability—

most always—on paper—it's the innocent party.

The insurance company is the collision casualty.

And the deer, having to occupy a planet with us,

are casualties of those and multiple other collisions.

Their only options are death or painful

healing processes. The real winners aren't
the insurance companies or the auto owners—
but the pampered wolves—well protected and fed.
The insurance companies camouflage
and deny their involvement. Why? *I ask.*
Because, *he says,* they have to sell insurance
to farmers, hunters, and pet owners. *As usual,*
I nod and wonder—because unlike the babied, tried,
and practiced notions seemingly
teetering on the verge of falling asleep or dying,
his are zingy, on their feet, racing with little direction
but a lot of zip. They misbehave—send you
to where you've never been, to keep company
with what you never have. This gives you a shot
to feel what you haven't felt, think what you
haven't thought, do what you haven't done.
After he leaves, I sit and have a few beers with a robust,
mollycoddled wolf—a manipulative insurance CEO,
an angry, maimed deer, and a maverick notion.

Deadpan Insurance Man

Sprouts and Thumbs

My Uncle Kerry—who just retired

from tramping the woods

for the U.S. Forest Service

for forty-some years—likes

to take trite sayings and wrap

them in provocative swabs

of the greenery of the forests

he loves. Just yesterday he says,

"Life is a penny. And a penny

ain't worth much nowadays;

they'll soon be obsolete."

"So what?" I ask. "Life will go on,"

he says. "But we'll have to deal

with it in higher denominations.

If we don't curtail the ascension

of denominations, life will trek on

without us. We'll have to turn

the planet over to those beings

who don't measure their worth

in soaring denominations

and are content to simply

maintain the planet." "Like who?'

I ask. "Beings," he says, "with tails,

claws, fins, wings. Better yet,"

he says, "like my niece, your sister,

the botanist, would say,

beings who perch on roots

and watch over their babies

who have sprouted

claws, fins, wings, tails—

and especially those

who have sprouted

highly educated,

potentially hazardous thumbs."

Possum

A flashing, feisty allure
that flourishes in forests
of social climates dares me.
I, like the small-brained
nonsocial animals that can't
(or refuse to) recognize
their images in mirrors,
am wary of the large-brained
social animals that can
(or think they can).
A desire prowls around me
like a dangerous predator.
I, feeble possum that I am,
play dead—dream that
I grow a mane, find courage.

Planet Earth: THE THREE INN KEEPERS

I roar, devour the desire.

A cold surge of consciousness

drives away pretend,

hangs me by my prehensile tail.

Upside-down, I watch,

through a pane of glass,

the orangutans, elephants, dolphins

admire, scrutinize their images

in assorted mirrors—

as the glowing allure

extinguishes itself

in a puddle of dull reflections.

Between a Canoe and a Dock

(For Lynn)

While lugging a disabled spirit,
I discover that the author of a poster
promoting my poetry reading calls
me a legend. Bang! My left brain pulls his nose
out of his *Bible of Established Objectivities*—
and cracks up—laughs so hard he has
to lie down and pound on the floor
of whatever chamber he hangs out in.
When he recovers, he pulls out the Pro-Flow,
500-pound test, five-inch diameter, low friction
fire hose he uses to pelt me with what he calls
"demonstrable actualities" and drenches me
with what "legend" likely means: The hose spouts,

Planet Earth: THE THREE INN KEEPERS

Legendary people are: (1) usually dead, (2) almost dead,
(3) should be dead, (4) flimsy products of myths,
(5) ordinarily two of the above. A delayed, stinging spurt

from the hose spouts, *People often become legendary*

when the tenure of their presence in people's lives

has been so offensive people can't shake

the memories of them—like Hitler or some

of our politicians. The drenching has my ailing spirit

helplessly treading water until my right brain

who, like always, instead of promptly reacting

to anything, sniffs around like a blood hound

in slow motion and finally, nonchalantly, drifts along

in the birch-bark vessel he—without plans or direction—

designed and hand crafted—and that looks like a cross

between a canoe and a dock. After I manage to climb in,

he paddles me over angry, defiant waters,

to those spacious wildernesses that are alive,

throbbing with freedom and feeling—where creativity

thrives. We dock on an exotic island where a hike

with the subjective phantom Intent leads me

to rare, persistent inspiration, thrusting me

into the challenge of exploration, discovery,

invention—and building.

As I work in that spacious wilderness,

a feeling deep in my bowels says, *This is where*

a hell-bent reflection was struggling to dock

you all along. And, suddenly, I humbly realize

it's the author of the Poster and its renegade tag—

"legend"—that resuscitates and gives my spirit

the energy to seat and paddle me from a fallow beach

of tame uniformity over angry, resistant waters

to land me on a provocative island of wild, alien

activity in the rebel vessel

that misbehaved, traveled forbidden

water courses: the cross

between a canoe—and a dock.

Legend

Shore

(For Grady)

They yell, *ENABLER* at me.
LEAVE YOUR KID ALONE. QUIT
MOLLYCODDLING HIM,
they scold. *HE HAS TO HIT BOTTOM.*
LET HIM DROWN OR SWIM TO SHORE.
Drugs, peers keep pulling, swirling him,
twain by twain, farther from shore. I keep tossing
the May West on a lifeline, pulling him back
until he opts to let go. Now, too far to swim back,
he flounders, sinks, surfaces. They yell louder,
LEAVE HIM ALONE. I can't. I throw the May
West,
jerk him in a ways—stop. He lets go. I drag it in; he

flounders, sinks, surfaces—flounders, sinks, surfaces.
I toss it again; he grabs it; I don't pull. He holds
awhile, lets go, flounders, sinks, surfaces—grabs it,
gets his wind, begins pulling hand over hand. I watch,
and tie the line to a tree. He lets go, flounders, grabs it
before he sinks—hand over hand—stronger pull.
He stops, rests, waves to me, flings the May West
and—amid their cheers, my tears—swims to shore.

Camping

My niece, an animal lover
and zoology major at the University,
reacts to a comment I make
about a feeling that the money
from my book sales and poetry readings are
mere personally consoling contributions
to the creative programs for area children
I'm attempting to establish and maintain.
She says, You're such a pessimist!
I say, Be careful. There are two major camps
between Camps Optimism and Pessimism:
Camps Indifference and Realism. Camp Optimism
and Camp Pessimism are where quitters
and cowards vacation. Believing things
are all good or bad cancels doubt—

the life blood of exploration, discovery,

creativity. Camp Indifference kills action.

Camp Realism, the smallest camp,

demands exploration, discovery, thought—

and action. Now, *I ask her,* where do you

intend to stick me? *She gives me her*

I'm-searching-my-animal-menagerie look.

Her face tells me she's caught something.

Finally she says, You're in a tent.

They won't let you into any of the camps.

You're outrageous, demented.

In your lonely wanderings, you run into hikers

from other camps. They shun you.

The pessimists sometimes acknowledge you

with a nod or a wave. *She nods her head*

and waits for me to react. I attempt

to put together a meaningful reaction;

I quickly give up and say, That is one

cockamamie analogy! You concocted it

to addle, agitate—hamstring both chambers

of my brain. HEY! *She yells.* IF YOU CAN USE

METAPHORS TO FUCK WITH MY MIND,

I CAN USE THEM TO FUCK WITH YOURS.

I nod. You're right. I'm not a happy camper.

She smiles, says, Cheer up. The animals

tolerate you. *I smile. From her,*

that's a huge compliment. And you? *I ask.*

Barely, *she says.* The animals swung me.

They formed a committee, sealed the deal

and recommended tolerance. *When I don't let go*

of my smile, she says, It was a five-to-four vote.

Inflatable

Like a gripping overdose
of Xanax, Futility rushes
in and envelopes me—
in a punctuating, suffocating
stress that deflates
the uplifting stress
of Feasibility. Futility collapses
me—mooring me in
the flat comfort of inaction.
I suffer the submission
until Intolerance ignites
anger, determination,
energy returns, and adrenaline
gusts through me. Soon,
like a wild, threatened animal,

Feasible barges in and raises hell,

driving Futile away, returning

rousing stress that sends me

back to work, shouting

inspiration, exploration,

discovery, and *application.*

The dynamic stress pumps me,

takes me to wildernesses

to find my way and gather

figments to build vehicles

to deliver my meager

but sincere bursts of hot air

to the deflated, potentially

productive segments

of creativity deprived, drugged,

collapsing cultures who will forgive

my trespass and allow me to hope

my tiny bursts of helium

might give them a lift.

Bridges

The guy sitting next to me

at the Keystone Bar in the tiny village

of Ramsay, Michigan sticks

a cigarette in his mouth

and gets up to go outside.

The woman sitting on the other side

of him grabs his sleeve, looks up

at him, and says, "Honey, I wish

you wouldn't." He laughs, looks

at me apologetically and says,

"The little wife." He pulls his arm away

from her grip and heads

to the door. Two more at the bar

get up, pop cigarettes in their mouths

and head out to join him. His wife

looks at me with a sad smile and says,

"He's not well. The doctors have warned

him. We've begged him to quit."

She shrugs. I say, "Everyone should quit.

The evidence is overwhelming:

Smokers are debilitating and killing

themselves along with numerous

other people who are victims

of their hand-me-down smoke."

She nods, points at herself, and says,

"Like me." The guy on the other side

of me pokes me and says, "Hey!

Hold on. Like the name says,

This place is the keystone of Ramsay.

It holds people together. Leave it be."

I say, "I wasn't aware I was tampering

with it." He pokes a cigarette

in his mouth and says. "We smokers

need a stone to keep us from crumbling."

He walks outside. I look at the woman

on my left and shrug. An older man

who was sitting several stools away

walks over and says, "I've been listening in,

and I'd like to offer my thoughts."

I nod at him. He says. "There are

good reasons to consider The Keystone Bar

the keystone of Ramsay. The Keystone Bar

enables towns people with diverse interests,

struggling with diverse problems, concerns,

dilemmas, and crises to travel

over different bridges and cross

a single bridge they can share

to integrate and help each other better deal

with their lives by giving them

the incentive, courage, and energy

to stay strong and get stronger.

There are old retired people like me

about to run into the end of their lives;

there are debilitated people; there are

people who are lonely who need

to share their efforts and achievements
with people who have common interests—
like hunters, sports fans, fishermen, artists,
 politicians, and the like. Sure, some
of them reinforce bad habits.
But a lot of them help each other
kick them." He heads for the door;
with his hand on the door knob, he turns
and says, "I'm crossing the bridge
to join the smokers to see if I can
shoot down some of the bold, dangerous,
cockamamie reasoning processes
that they're usually flying by each other
out there." He closes the door
and the woman next to me says,
"Sounds good. But I think there's
more rationalizing and justifying their bad habits
out there than working on getting rid of them."
She points at the door and says,
"Larry's a retired vet. He's good for this place.

He's into alternative medicine, health food,

and exercise. He does make a difference,

but I think he rationalizes how much

of a difference he makes. He's

pretty idealistic." I say, "It shows

how rationalizing is not only a friend

of Debilitation but also Rehabilitation.

We rationalize to justify our misbehavior

but also to put more energy and time

into what we're doing to improve

our behavior and the behavior of others."

I jerk my thumb at the door and say,

"The Vet there . . ." She interrupts and inserts,

"Doc—we call him Doc." "Doc," I say, "has

to feel he's making a big difference

to keep plugging away the way

he evidently does." She nods and says,

"Right, I just seldom think of it that way."

Doc, the vet, who went out

to shoot down dangerous reasoning

processes comes in waving a sheet

of paper. I ask, "How was your aim?"

He laughs and says, "By the way,

I used ammunition from—" he points

at me and the woman next to me—

"your and your discussion, that I

eavesdropped on, to score

my biggest hit. Just to give you an idea

of the bizarre notions and whims

I often battle with, listen to this.

Big Fred, who just returned

from one of his trips to Vegas,

is out front handing out fliers

from a Vegas bar and grill where he hangs out

called The Heart Attack Grill." Doc reads

from the flier: *"Over 350 pounds? Eat free.*

And on the menu: 8,000 calorie

Octuple Bypass Burger w/ 40 bacon slices;

½ Pound Coronary Dog; from the bar:

a 3.5 oz. Whipped cream Vodka; and
from their one-item Vegan menu—he jerks
his thumb at the door—
they really ran with this one: Salad: 100%
Leaf Tobacco—No meat additives."
I laugh, look at Doc and say, "It's a joke—
right?" He says, "No, it's a real bar and grill
sending lots of people to early debilitation and death.
It was just a short while ago
they had their first customer die
of a heart attack while at the bar and Grill.
They're celebrating him as a hero."
I shake my head as the guy, who
was sitting next to me and started
all this, returns and slides somberly
onto his stool. He forces a smile,
hands his wife his pack of cigarettes,
and says, "Put these out of commission
for me please." She says, "Honey,
you're not really? . . ." She wipes tears

from her eyes. "Cold turkey," he says.

"I'm done." She throws her arms around him

and sobs softly on his shoulder. I look at Doc.

He smiles and nods. The guy yells

over his wife's head, "Hey Doc! When you get

a chance, turn me on to a good exercise

and diet routine. I'm in terrible shape."

Doc says, "Anytime." Then the guy turns

to the bartender and says, "No more shots and ale.

Let me try one of those"—he points at my beer—

"64-calorie low-alcohol sissy beers

that Miller puts out." As I get up to leave,

he grabs my sleeve and nods at me.

I nod back and hold out my hand; he grabs it

with both of his and gives it a squeeze

that radiates gratitude. I leave gripping

the gratitude and take the short walk

to the Ramsay Keystone Bridge. I sit

and ponder my adventures with bridges—

take a close look at bridges I've travelled

and a closer look at those I hadn't

the courage to cross. Then I head back

to continue pondering over a few

of those 64-calorie, low-alcohol sissy beers—

at—Yep—The Keystone Bar.

Keystone Bridge, Ramsay, Michigan

33

Keystone Bar, Ramsay, Michigan

Verse in Need of Revision

Some editor

told me to "hammer it out,"

said it needed

some straightening

and direction, didn't like

 the irregularities—

the turns and stops

that shouldn't be there

he said. And I tried,

but the hammer

was wrong—

like The Grand Twins

of the Twin Grands,

Ferrante and Teicher,

with a set of cymbals

or Picasso with a spray gun

I guess.

So I gave the hammer

to a grateful scholar

and caused

this poem instead.

Endangered

Cultures often declare
open seasons on the wrong
things. While it's difficult
for me to accept that it's
logical to kill anything,
I know there are exceptions.
Cultures dictate to us
what we can kill,
what we must kill, and
what we can't kill.
I console myself by not killing
things I can or things
the culture tells me
I should. But one animal
they pay bounties on

and declare a wide-open season

for is an animal we have

no right to kill. It's the ultimate

endangered species: *Our Time*.

We ought to be doing everything

we can to ensure our Time's longevity—

which, understated, is brief.

But cultures are good at altering

its real mission and camouflaging

the alteration. They corral it

and ride it to carry out

the cultures' missions instead

of the individuals' missions.

Time is a clever, valuable animal.

It keeps attempting

to alert us of its brief visit

and invaluable presence.

In the culture's control, it

too often plays tricks on us.

Sometimes we yearn to zap

it and it stands strong,

invincible. We curse it.

Then at the damndest times

when we need it, it rolls

over and plays dead—

and we curse it. Suddenly,

it resurrects just soon enough

to hurry us—and we blunder,

cursing it for resurrecting.

If there's any earthly entity

that belongs on the endangered species list,

it's Our Time—our most exotic,

valuable critter.

Droppings

My niece, a zoology student
at the University, bursts
into my office and starts ranting
about people who have no knowledge
of the behavior of animals or respect
for them—even the human kind.
She says, I was just at the Clinton River
Nature Center Park and there was
a woman feeding the geese.
She was standing right next to a sign
that was nearly pleading with visitors
not to feed the water fowl. *I ask,*
What's wrong with feeding water fowl?
She gives me her mother, my sister's
you-stupid-fucker look, *says,* The feeding

of the water fowl causes the birds to lose

their instinct of migration and become

permanent residents. Large congregations

of water fowl stir up large amounts

of siltation that suffocate and kill

endangered clams that inhabit

the Clinton River. The droppings

of large congregations of water fowl

germinate a fungal disease that causes

histoplasmoss in humans. *I say,* Even

if they did care about and respect animals,

most people aren't likely to run into any

of that information. *She says,* It says on the sign

it can cause serious contagious consequences

that affect both humans and other animals.

I read the sign to her. And? *I ask. She gave me*

the look *and kept on feeding. I say,* I think

animal droppings are an element humans

would rather ignore. And yet, *she says,*

as you told me years ago when you had me

forking chicken shit on my mother's

vegetable garden, they're vital to life

on the planet. Wait a minute, *I say.*

It was the botanist, my sister, your mother,

the straw boss, who had you forking manure.

She says, But it was your chicken shit; it came

from your chickens. *I say,* It was a gift

for my sister. You just got hooked into

the application process. Okay, *she says,*

I'll blame Mom. *She laughs.* Remember you

told her it was too young? It needed a year

to mellow or it would burn her seeds

and the roots of her seedlings—and she bet

you a steak dinner it wouldn't. *I nod.* And?

she asks. I smile, say, I bought. *My niece says,*

My mom knows her shit—*pauses*—

too well sometimes. And her plants.

And she knows how to use them to smother

otherwise carefree, stress-free existence.

It's why I'm sweating away at the University

instead of spending more time enjoying

and befriending my animal friends

in the fields, woods, swamps. *I say,*

You should post a sign and read it aloud

to your mom. *She gives me* the look,

says, She'd only give me *the look.*

Grey Gloves Finals

Frugal fights Generous

and wins by a TKO

in the third round.

Cheap steps into the ring

and, on a split decision,

defeats Frugal.

In the fight for the championship,

Greedy cold-cocks Cheap

in the seventh round.

The referee raises

Greedy's right arm, yells,

"CHAMP**EE**ION" and Greedy

proudly retires

to an exclusive

retirement resort

for dignitaries where,

wallowing in overindulgence

and waste, he celebrates

throughout the rest

of his hollow life

like a lazy retired frog*

in the sludge

of a stagnant leisure.

*If there was a retirement program

 for frogs or such a thing as lazy frogs.

Carved in Ice

I sit with a priest who has forbid
members of his congregation to enroll
in any of my classes. I can't determine
if anger, compassion, or curiosity sent him—
or if he's simply recruiting. I've sorted
through brambles of his rhetoric,
located concrete nouns and verbs,
and decided he's just asked me
if I believe in a supreme being.

I don't know, I say, But from what
I can get together I strongly doubt it.

That's a cop out, he says. You either have
to believe it or disbelieve it.

Planet Earth: THE THREE INN KEEPERS

I never have enough evidence
to believe or disbelieve anything.
There are too many variables—
everything's constantly changing,
bombarding me with contrary evidence.

So you never believe anything?

That's right—or disbelieve anything.
Belief and disbelief are really
different faces of the same ghost.

So how firm are those things you doubt least?

I decide to play payback with my own
rhetorical brambling. I say,
Early last March on a spring-like day
like today, I tried to explain it to a lit class
and found myself foundering in a metaphor.

I'll give you a shot at it. Those things
that are feeble doubts—that I miscall
my beliefs—I carve in blocks of ice,
try to ignore them, and leave them
to the mercy of fickle Upper Michigan
early March temperatures.
Those things that I doubt more severely
I carve in blocks of ice, hunt for answers.
Then I let new evidence that I scare up
move them back and forth
from early march into mid-April.

That's decadent, he says.
You need strong faith.

Faith is dangerous; it slams shut
thought processes. We have
to be careful. Everything
we are and need is carved in ice—
at the mercy of the planet's

central climate control system

that a universe, that doesn't give

a dead man's rap, installed and operates.

The look he gives me says the metaphor

melted away along with my other words.

That look bothers me for a few seconds

until I remember I got a whole class room

full of the same looks last March.

Easter, Maybe

After I miss an Easter date with her
and after she finishes yowling threats
and accusations, my girl calms, says,
You're good at pretending not to notice things.
I don't pretend, *I say.* I do make efforts *not*
to notice things—and sometimes it works.
Besides, I didn't forget our date; I forgot
it was Easter. I did remember it was almost Easter
on Tuesday for a little while because it meant
I wouldn't have classes on Friday and Saturday.
I remembered it for a while after I got your e-mail
Wednesday, then I forgot about it until late Easter
and remembered only because I was reflexively
going about putting in my usual work-study shift
until I noticed the teachers who come in
to work late Sunday didn't show. That, too late,

sent my mind back to the email and Easter.

You'll find comfort in that, no matter how hard

I tried, I couldn't stop noticing it was Easter the rest

of the day. I realize my memory lapses are likely due

to dead brain cells or cells that were never there

and should be or cells that shouldn't be there.

My mind's always behaved this way—

as well as I can remember. As well as I can

remember, *she says*, you've always

remembered to go to work, never missed

a fishing outing with your buddies,

always kept appointments. And you were

never even late for a date with me

back when hormones were cracking the whip.

If you remember, *I say,* those were the hormones

you told me to kick out of the catbird seat—

drive my own team of horses. That, *she says,*

was before I realized what a wimp of a driver

I'd get. Give the seat and the whip

back to the hormones.

The Chase

(A College English Professor
Almost Outruns Her Students)

Her career was a chase.

Like merciless phantom ferrets

students charged

from her subconscious.

But she flourished on the battle.

She was captain

of her own forces, the strategist

of her campaign.

That she relied upon rapid

and frequent strategic withdrawal

was academic. Victory,

to her had become

a matter of elusiveness.

Then one day her Career

staggered, fell, and was dead.

The ferrets swarmed

over her and gloated—

until the stench of the dead

sent them to where Youth

and Challenge were calling.

Shrugging off her laments,

she thought it strange

that she should be thinking back

to when she was a supporter

of the ferret militia—when she used

to believe that, instead of pioneers,

Emerson and Thoreau were radicals.

A Lonely Ex-Boxer's Revelation

Suffering can be

a wisdom warrior.

He can lambaste

and arouse victims

with rare inspiration,

exploration, and discovery—

but only when Suffering victims

have the courage to step

into the ring with him—

and when Strength, Energy,

Open-mindedness,

and Love are their trainers

and in their corners advising

and administering—

preparing them

for round after round

of battling challengers

of individualism,

free thought, and action.

Clock Work

Without tiny machines
waving hands, flashing digits—
ringing, buzzing—mandating—
the sun, the moon, and seasons
still keep their appointments.
The tide, the plants,
the nonhuman animals,
unhurried, follow their lead,
content and on time
for their engagements.

It seems as though
Human nature casts and directs
a parody. In search of freedom
and peace of mind, we, the players,

Planet Earth: THE THREE INN KEEPERS

rush to invent restraints

and sentence ourselves

to the confining security

of command, violence,

and confusion—

where we race and rage

around the lockup—

chasing nothing—to nowhere.

One of a Kind; One of Many Kinds

Character and Personality
are not twins; they're
from diversely different
cultures. They have little
in common and tangle
with each other. Character
is often crude, offensive,
unpredictable—sincere
and honest—a rare renegade.
Personality is typical, polite,
sophisticated, and popular—
a showoff. Character runs
people through tough
conditioning programs
that prepare them

for grueling expeditions

and propels them, all alone,

down rugged trails to explore,

discover, and create. Personality

chauffeurs them like celebrities

down the easy highways

to rehearse, imitate, and perform.

Vacationland

Obstacles try

like hell

to make friends

with me.

They convincingly

invite me

to enter

the mellow retreat

of Excuse

and Escape

where my efforts

metamorphose

into deviations

that ride

on leisure,

blocking entry

to a world

of determination

where Challenge

inspires me

and demands

I barrel

into the obstacles

—conquer them,

file them in the past,

and drive myself

to trek though

the demanding terrain

beyond them

to pursue

singular goals

that deep

in my bowels wait—

daring me

to discover, rescue,

and share them.

Friends can be

cloaked obstacles

who intentionally

or inadvertently

divert me

from enduring deep,

rugged wildernesses,

raging waters,

turbulent, erupting skies

to explore

and discover

to find

the way and means

to be who I

have the ability

and strength to be.

My obsessive craving

for friendship

is common.

Planet Earth: THE THREE INN KEEPERS

Unfortunately,

reflexively,

without thought,

I too often

use friends

to help me justify

avoiding confronting

and overcoming

the obstacles

and instead

I retreat

to the mellow

Vacationland

of Excuse and Escape—

where they cleverly

metamorphose

into the mellow

vacationland

of Fulfillment

that they have tricked

me to believe I

have diligently

fought for and duly

earned and where I'll

find happiness

beyond what I've

ever experienced.

The reality is

those of us

who eventually escape

will look back

and see

the Vacationland

as a dump ground

and wasteland

where we scrapped

the seeds and sprouts

of our incentives

that will never

see or feel

the sun and rain

of Application

or know

the cultivation

of Caring. We'll

struggle

with the revelation

that our exclusive

seeds and sprouts

will never bloom

or bear fruit—

knowing that they

would have yielded

crops to flourish

and nourish others

as well as ourselves—

had we not condemned

them to die and rot

in the mellow Vacationland

of Excuse and Escape.

Declarative

After lobster, wine, and sex,

gazing into each other's eyes,

he snaps his Zippo, holds the flame

to her cigarette. Like the brief flicker

of the brusque flame, like these words—

in this order—their love, health, and lives

plummet to the final period.

Herbivores and Carnivores

Since I was a kid,
I watched Harry,
an old retired Great Lakes
Sea Captain, deal
with what most people
in our community called
an anti-social, dangerous complex.
As I look back on it, it seems
to me that he became nauseated
and retreated whenever people
tried to force their sophistication
on him. And people would say
things like: "After all,
we're just being polite or nice
or friendly and he ignores us";

and to all of us kids:

"Stay away from that man;

he's dangerous"; our parents

forbid all of us from associating

with him. Fortunately,

the Community condemnation

and blackballing never cured Harry.

His "complex" drove him alone

to a world of meaning and creativity.

Instead of gallivanting

around the Community social world

of parties, celebrations,

and other superficial activities,

he spent his time with his dog

and wife—gardening, maintaining

a small fruit orchard, fishing,

and wood crafting—sharing

the fruits of his efforts

with whoever could use them.

I was one of the few kids

lucky enough to be able

to disobey my parents

and get away with it. I spent

some of my most memorable

and fruitful hours and days

with Harry—fishing

in his canvas boat on Pontiac Lake,

helping him with his gardening,

crafting, and fruit orchard.

(He paid me well and I

sometimes would give a dollar

or so to some of the kids

of the parents who we delivered

to or who came to the house

for his wares).

What Harry gave me

that has camped deep within me

since I first met him is invaluable.

We first bonded when he caught

me stealing apples from his orchard.

He helped me down from the tree.

We ate an apple and later walked

to his berry patch and ate

some raspberries while he told

stories of his experiences

on the Great Lakes and introduced

me to his Sheltie Shepard dog Blizzard.

I tried to give the apples back

I had stuffed in my pockets,

but he shook his head and instead

got me a bag and filled it for me

to take home.

And now I still practice

at getting nauseas

at sophistication. But it's

a struggle. Like the carnivore

who can't develop a taste

for herbage, my appetite

for people makes it difficult.

And so I continue to struggle

against becoming rich,

well-fed, respected, and sterile.

I find my mind sends me where

I should be going and doing

what I should be doing

when it's grazing on herbage

of sacrifice and giving—

instead of chomping on the meat

of self-gratification.

As painful as grazing on the herbage

sometimes is, I can't find

anything in chomping

the carnivore diet that produces

the sense of wellbeing

like grazing and being able

to feel that I've made

contributions to the wellbeing
of others—and maybe even
encouraged a few to graze—
instead of chomp.

Roots, Feathers, Skin, Fur, Scales—
and a Poem

My niece, an animal activist
pursuing a career in zoology,
bangs into my office and slaps
a folder on my desk. I look at it,
then at her. Giving me my sister,
the botanist, her mother's
"You-dumb-fucker look,"
she says, *Well,* open it." I open it
and take a poem from the top
of some other papers and hold it
up to her. She nods and says,
"It's a poem for my freshman comp class.
It's supposed to rhyme. I argued
with the teacher, but she stuck

to outlawing free verse. She said
rhyming is good writing discipline."
"So?" I ask. "So read the damn poem
and tell me if it qualifies." "Qualifies
for what?" She gives me
her mother's "look" again, and says,
"Rhyming!" I read the poem, look at her,
shrug, and say, "I had to search,
but I found some semblance
of rhyming." She nods and says,
"She wants it to rhyme more—
at the end of each line." I nod.
She says, "This is all your damn fault."
"My fault?" "Yeah, your philosophical
influence that has been warping
my mind since I was a child." "Like?"
"Like," she says, "there is no rhyme
or reason to reality. So it follows
that rhyme slaughters the reality
in poetry." I nod. "So," she says, "help
me fix this poem without slaughtering

the reality." I read the poem again,

nod, and say, "Easy." "How?" She asks.

I say, "I found three key words

that rhyme. So simply make it

a three-line poem with those words

at the end of each line." She gives me

her mother's You-stupid-fucker look.

I shrug and wait for words. Finally, she

laughs and says, "They'll be awful long lines.

But show me. I know the three words,

but what'll it look like?" She sits

at my computer. We format the poem

in Three rhyming stanzas instead

of lines. "OK," she says—"we'll try it—

on one condition." "What's that?"

"If she gives me a low grade on it,

you have to go with me to help me

yell at her—like you did that time

I snuck that controversial article

in the high school paper and they

tried to expel me from school."

"Yeah," I say, we won that one." "Did we ever!"
she says. "And the article even got printed
in the *Metro Daily Globe* after the battle
was over, and it had a huge audience."
She laughs again. "That sure was fun!
It was one time I was thankful you
warped my mind with your
no-rhyme-or-reason thinking." "Maybe,"
I say, "it'll happen this time, and your poem
will end up in the *Metro Daily Globe*."
She laughs. "I wish! But this isn't controversy
that'll rile the people like my article did.
It's just a violation of a teacher's stupid rule.
The worst that can happen is I'll get
an "F" on it." She snatches her poem
off my desk, sticks it in her folder,
and heads for the door. She stops
at the door, turns, and says,
"I'm not going to thank you until I get
the verdict." Fair enough," I say.
She smiles, waves, and leaves.

A few days later my niece *bangs*

into my office, like she usually does,

and drops the poem on my desk.

I ask, "So?" In a cross tone, she asks,

"So what?" "So what's the verdict?" She gives

me her mother's you-stupid-fucker look,

points at the poem, and says,

in the same cross tone, "Look at the damn thing."

I pick up the poem, ignore the comments

in the margins, and turn it over

to find the grade. It's an "A-." "So?" I ask.

She points at me and says, "You realize

that's the lowest grade I ever got

in an English class." "So?" I ask. "SO WHAT?"

she yells. "So does that mean we go to battle

over a minus?" She almost smiles, trying

to hold on to the same cross tone,

she says, "Naw, the poem would never

make the *Metro Daily Globe* anyway.

And the teacher was nice to me and my poem

in the margins." I read the comments—

all positive except the one above the grade:

"'These aren't lines; they're stanzas!' "

"She really liked your poem," I say. She nods,

takes the poem from me, turns, walks out,

and closes the door. A few seconds go by

and she opens the door, steps in and says,

"I forgot something." I wait. "*Thanks!*" she says.

I nod. She smiles and says, "I really mean it."

"The thanks or the smile?" I ask. "Both,"

she says. "And that goes for helping me

with the poem *and* for warping

my mind and turning me into

a no-rhyme-or-reason dissident—trekking

among the plants and animals,

under the skies, over the land, and the waters

of the planet. I love it. I mean it." She smiles.

I can feel her penetrating sincerity

from across the room, and it nearly

brings tears to my eyes. She waves,

says bye, and turns to leave. I decide

to lighten it up a bit. I call her.

She turns, still smiling. I say, "You ought
to change your major from Zoology
to Drama." Her smile widens; she flips me
a friendly bird, laughs, and leaves me
with more energy, inspiration,
and determination than I've had
in months—probably ever since the last time
she rejuvenated my mind with some of her
Inn Keepers of the Planet—animal/plant—
sky-soil-and-water therapy.

The Poem:

Soil, Water, and Sky:

generate the energy,
provide the living
and the dying accommodations
for tenants that bud, bloom,
crawl, walk, swim, and fly.

We human beings establish
ourselves as superior,
point our noses at the sky,
wander, flounder, and trek among
the planet's many mysteries,
assaults, and temptations
till we—reluctantly—die.

These are not lines;

they're stanzas!

A-

A Judge of Character

When Aunt Margaret
divorced Uncle Jed,
he assured the judge
he'd fulfill certain
Marital-type obligations—
plus paying alimony.
When the judge asked
how he expected to do it
in divorce when he
couldn't do it
in marriage, Uncle Jed
said, "You can't expect
a carrier pigeon
to deliver—unless you
let it out of the cage."

Damned if the judge
didn't understand!

The Train and the Scrapper

Disappointment lurks
in the caboose
of Pleasure's luxury train.
When we book a ride
with Pleasure, a stately,
cheerful usher, who bubbles
with promises of thrills
and merriment, shuttles us
not to the dining car
but to the caboose,
where Disappointment
attacks us and normally kicks
our asses. We have to stay
in training—keep in shape, K.O.
the scrappy fellow.

The caboose guy Disappointment

is just doing his job.

He's not unreasonable

or destructive. He's talented.

He loves his work and takes

his job seriously; he trains rigorously—

stays in shape. We can learn a lot

from him. The fight's good for us.

It can keep us alert—sharpen

our senses, build our resolve.

Brutally harsh Disappointment

can be a redeemer. Wade in swinging.

Win some fights, lose some.

Recruit the spoils of the victories

and defeats to find the courage

to abandon the train,

to trek into the wildernesses alone—

and get to work. Explore, discover,

invent. When we can, let's stay away

from chauffeured vehicles

like trains, trek into wildernesses

of challenges and revelations,

and thrive on achievement

and stay in charge

of our own directions

and destinations. Let's travel

with commitments, sacrifices,

and dedication and run

our psyches through nourishment

and conditioning programs—

get them in shape, climb

in the ring with Disappointment—

and win. Then, enlist the victory

to inject the inspiration

and energy to send our lives

and the lives of others back

to expeditions to explore

and discover. This gives us

a shot to use our revelations

and creations to help

combat the control

and destruction rushing

across our planet that's

extinguishing well-being

and jeopardizing existence.

Derby

Humans are the reasoning animals,
which gives us the ability
to reason irrationally
and rationally. We can
distinguish between right
and wrong and choose
to do either. And
when we choose wrong,
we're capable of and clever
at rationalizing it as right.
We conclude that the gift
of reasoning makes
us superior to all other living
and inanimate forms
of existence. We use

Planet Earth: THE THREE INN KEEPERS

the same cockamamie

reasoning to make

distinctions within our species

to justify abusing and killing

each other to groom our Greed

like a champion steed,

celebrate our victories,

reap the financial, social,

and political spoils of the losers.

Then we train, groom—and trailer

our Greed to the next derby

and place long-shot bets.

Factory Farm

Scholarly Thinking celebrates
and employs thought as
an ingestion-egestion process—
bypassing feeling. Its mechanics,
dominantly objective, suppress
emotion and independent thought
and attack doubt, exploration,
discovery, and change. It captures
and commits Feeling to a factory farm
where it can no longer free-range—
where cruel, confining cages built
of facts, rules, customs, and traditions
ban Feeling from Thought and kill
independence and doubt—prohibiting
creativity. Helplessly, painfully,

Planet Earth: THE THREE INN KEEPERS

Feeling suffers imprisonment—

wistfully enduring the neglect,

the waste—waiting

for those rare raids that Courage

and Care operate to bust

through Scholarly Thinking's

disciplined defenses, releasing Feeling

from the confinement of the cages

and corrals to run, roam, sail—

the prairies, seas, forests

of the unexplored. Unshackled

and free, Feeling calls

the forces of Independent Thought

to battle hate and violence—

putting emotion and Creativity

back to work—resurrecting

crucified love and peace.

Good Eye

I meet Jim at the Ramada Inn.

He's interviewing me

for a position at the college

where he chairs the Board.

We went to school,

played ball together.

He set the record for walking,

I for striking out.

It's my second try to stay

on base as an English teacher.

The first administration

caught me running

reckless innovations,

giving students alien visions

that encouraged them

to think and doubt.
My lead-off from third base
was a little too bold—
and they picked me off.

He sips wine and tells me
about the fortune
he's made with his chain
of hardware stores,
shakes his head at my story
of foul balls and strike outs.
He lectures me:
Caution is the key—discretion.
You remember my bailiwick
was walking. I didn't go
for the bad balls.
I had a good eye.
It's been that way since.
I've learned to let
doubtful balls go

rather than swing and fan.
It's what I don't rush into
that makes sense,
gives me the most returns.

I shrug, swig my beer. I stand,
grab an empty snack plate,
set it on the floor behind him.
He turns—watches.
I pick up an imaginary "bat,"
begin swinging it around.
Loosening my shoulders,
I say, I've been beating air
since little league.
A couple times I super slammed.
I wouldn't trade those two hits
for walks or trophies or money.

I take my stance, move my "bat"
across the plate three times—

wait—swing. I shade

my eyes with my hand, say,

Number three's still out there.

His laugh jerks over his shoulder,

quivers in mid air—

like an umpire's thumb.

Duck

Duck, *she says. I look around.* Where? *I ask.*
She says, No, "duck"—the verb. Look
the fuck out. I'm about to fire some
high-powered shit at you. Shouldn't
you be shooting at the ducks? *I ask.*
The verb, asshole. "Shoot" *is* a verb, *I say.*
No, "duck," *she says.* Where? *I ask.*
The VERB, *she screams.* The verb "duck,"
I say. Action verb, right? RIGHT, *she screams.*
Or state of being? *I ask. She says,*
If you don't get serious, your state
of being is in deep shit. Shit? *I ask.* Verb?
Noun, asshole. Fuck, *I say. Her voice drops*
several decibels. Noun or verb? *she asks.*
Both, *I say. She smiles. My lampoonery*

finally annoyed her animosity
to submission. As she slips out
of her blouse she says, Duck fuck.
"Verb," *I say. She says,* You finally got it.
She drops her jeans, says, Action.

Alternativeness:

Tools and Paths

By Twos

An artist uses two different color combinations to create the same overtone and mood in the same painting.

Each of two carpenters use different tools to make the same repair on damaged garage doors.

Two men use different spiels to seduce the same woman.

A bandit uses two different schemes to pilfer money from the same source.

Two doctors use different therapies to spawn the same recovery.

In the following two poems, a narrator plays a song that sends the same message on two different instruments—the first poem on his oboe; the second poem on his saxophone.

As you read the two poems, allow the tones and pitches of the oboe and of the sax to foster musical overtones and innuendos that set exclusive moods for each poem.

Rough Route

To instruct is *not* to educate.
Instruction dictates directions,
steers us down super highways
to defined destinations;
education turns us loose
in pristine wildernesses
to forage our own paths
and explore, discover, capture
what only we can preserve
and share. It's a creative adventure—
not an ingestion-regurgitation tour.
Be wary of instruction; it often rides
with indoctrination. Give courage
a shout. When he barrels in,
grab him, hang on. Enter

the unexplored land of Real Education.

Take chances. Fight your way

to revelations that will make

positive differences in yours

and others' lives. It's a painful process

that demands integrity, inspiration,

dedication: an expedition that hands

slackers and cowards maps that lead

them back to the super highways.

Introduction to a Myth

Real education is a well-trained,

obedient regiment of comfortable,

objective problem-solving forums drilling

to collaborative beats of popular institutions.

Real education is not rugged, savory adventure

where Doubt sends us all alone to confront

the obscure, unexplored wildernesses

of experience. It's not what puts us to work

where we become acquainted

with the notion that we don't

understand anything. It's not where we solo

and rely on and extend only *our* exclusive

mental and physical faculties to their limits.

All that and the outlandish notion

that real education is where

we search, discover, decipher,

invent—create what no one else can—

to deliver, heal, and improve

in a way no one else has

is all pure nonsense.

A Tale of Dishes

Dishes are tattle tales, I say, as I look
at the four the waitress just scattered
in front of me—plus the one with salad
she laid down twenty minutes ago.
How so? My seventeen-year-old niece asks,
as she finishes working on her salad.
They tell revealing stories about squander,
integration, and separatism. I pull
the large dish with the main course
in front of me, then from the four dishes,
I scrape the salad that I haven't touched;
the vegetable; the baked potato;
the cranberry sauce and biscuit all
on the large dish. I stack
the four empty dishes

and begin to eat.

She shakes her head and smiles.

Then she scrapes

the remaining food

from her four small dishes

on to the large dish, stacks

them next to mine, gives me

one of her rare looks

where her eyes

flitter scattered applause,

and begins to eat.

Witching

My mother and father,

their friends and relatives,

keep asking each other

how my Uncle Henry,

who works for the US Forest Service,

has a Diary Farm, and operates

a fishing-guide business, has lived

so long and why he works so hard

at his three jobs and doesn't retire

or at least take it easy,

like his three brothers and all

of his other relatives and friends

who are years and years younger

than him. I ask my mom why she

doesn't ask him. She laughs and says,

"He's way too difficult to talk to.

When you ask him a question, he'll just

go off on some abstract word tangent

that'll make you sorry you asked it."

I tell her when I ask him questions

he doesn't do that. She tells me

I'm a little too young to realize it.

So I decide to ask him. I find him

out by his barn splitting wood.

I catch his eye. He nods, smiles,

and takes a few more swings

with his ax before he leans it

against the barn. He points

at the scattered split wood and begins

to stack it on an already huge pile.

I hurry and help him until we have it

all neatly stacked. He turns to me,

nods, and asks, "What's up kid?"

I decide to be point blank. I say,

"Mom and every one are always asking

how you live so long, work so hard,

and don't retire or take it easy

like everyone else." He laughs and says,

"Remember the time I took you

with me during the drought a couple

of summers ago to dowse for water

so the township crew could find water

to drill for?" "Yeah," I say. "But we called it

witching for water." "That we did,"

he says. "That's because too many people

think that dowsing is magic

that only witches possess. What it really is,

I believe, is simply being in tune

with the life blood of the planet."

"How do we get in tune with the blood

of the planet?" I ask. "You simply shed

all of your immediate concerns

and thoughts and concentrate as hard

as you can on what you're attempting

to discover." I pretend to understand,

nod my head, and say. "I remember

you used a stick that wiggled

at the ground where the water was."

"That was a willow branch,"

he says. "Remember, the branch is a part

of the tree involved in sending messages

to the roots directing them

to the water the tree needs to survive."

"So it wiggles when you're holding

it over water?" I ask. "It bends, twitches,

points," he says. I'm not really sure

I understand, but I at least follow

what he's saying. I nod and say, "I see."

"Okay," he says. "Now imagine

I have a willow branch that, for as long

as I can remember, has been stuck

in a chamber of my brain." I

laugh and say, "Okay." He says,

"It's like dowsing, witching—

looking for water with forked willow branches.

It's like when the branches sense
where the water is and send the roots
there to take advantage of it.
My forked willow branch does
its witching in the right chamber of my brain,
where it twitches and points and sends me
to places that are painfully tough
to get to and even tougher to tolerate
once I get there. It's how I survive—
enduring the hardships of where
it sends me and realizing what I have
accomplished has not only made me
a better person but has also helped
others become better and happier people."
When I try to explain to my mom
what he said, she laughs and says,
"I told you so; forget it. It's not worth
bothering with." Her reaction bothers me
and it doesn't. I decide to stuff
the willow branch and my mom's indifference

in the past and forget about them.
But off and on until I went away to college,
Uncle Henry, I think unconsciously,
witched for me with his willow branch.
And now, years later, I have a willow branch
stuck in the right chamber of my mind.
And, like Uncle Henry's branch, my branch
sends me to places that challenge me
to get to them. After exhausting treks
to the destinations, the hard work
demands extreme mental and physical exertion,
perseverance, and dedication.
The trips and the ensuing endeavors
are time consuming and painful—
and produce the fruit of beautiful assurances
that battling and conquering the challenges
of the experiences has helped others
become better people and has made me
a better person. The overall witching scenario
has made me aware that staying alive

to witch as long as I can is worth

everything I can put into it. I'm afraid now

I'm going to live even longer

than Uncle Henry, who died

at a hundred-and-three just after

finishing splitting and piling

the winter supply of wood

for his granddaughter, who lived

alone and suffered from bouts

with arthritis. Mom, who died at seventy

in a nursing home, never gave Uncle Henry's

Willow Branch or my Willow Branch

a chance to introduce themselves.

She never got to know them.

But just before she died, having

difficulty speaking, she said to me,

"You know that witching willow branch

your Uncle Henry and you carry around

in your heads?" I nod and say, "Yeah."

"You tell your Uncle Henry and I'm telling you

that I wish I'd had a willow branch

in some chamber of my tiny mind

to do some witching with." She smiled at me

and winked before she fell into a coma.

Three nurses and two doctors worked

to revive her. Finally one doctor looked

at me, shook his head, and said "I'm afraid she's

gone"; the other doctor nodded. Just then

she moved, popped partially up,

looked at me, and said, like she might

have rehearsed it and just had

to come back to share it, "Witch some wells

for me that'll bubble with love, caring,

well-being, and *Action*. With the word *Action*

still on her lips, she managed a smile

and dropped back to the bed in a coma

that she never resurrected from—

but that more than doubled my intention

to use the witching branch Uncle Henry

gave me and many more times than

doubled my inspiration and energy to,

for the rest of my life, witch for

and dig wells that bubble

with love, caring, well-being, and *Action*.

Thanks, Mom. Thanks, Uncle Henry.

Fertile Flurries

Vanity and Pride, clever

Infiltrators into my world

of exploration

and endeavor, attack

me with tempting

and convincing

cultural productions

of established rules, laws,

customs, and traditions

that invite me to "retire"

to a supervised,

leisure-coated existence

of comfortable conformity.

My extensive recon to prepare

defenses to thwart

their attacks brings me

closer to Vanity's and Pride's

innate identities.

Vanity is how I struggle

to get other people

to see me. Pride is

how I struggle to see

myself. Neither changes

the innate me. Their strategy

is to eliminate "self,"

the guy I should be, primarily

by assassinating Humility.

I've discovered I have

to fight to protect the Humility

of being myself—ride

the winds, currents, waves;

trek the forests, prairies,

swamps of Humility's vigor

and provocation—let them

propel me into my exclusive,

pristine world to explore,

discover, and deliver

in fertile flurries

of self-reliant action—

without the pride-tainted

approval of Me

or the vanity-tainted

approval of Others.